This Book Belongs To:

_____

_____

_____

If you have any questions, comments or just want to say hello, please feel free to email me:
gisellemanaiza@yahoo.com

You can also connect with me on Instagram @myheartinwords_

This poetry-journal book is dedicated
to all those who believed in the gifts
that God gave me, even when I didn't.
Something beautiful blossomed
and for this I thank you.
-Giselle M.

My heart lies with the One who saved me.
He formed me with His hands,
He shaped me with His ways.
His breath gave me life,
even told me I was His prize.
Yet I lived in disguise,
always believed it was a lie
that a God so grand in size,
saw me perfect in His eyes.

Until the moment that I understood,
the majesty of His splendor
the love that was too much to measure,
my heart became at rest
and secretly confessed
that this is where I must remain
for I have found the One Who saved me.

Date: _____

Reflections: _____
_____
_____
_____
_____
_____
_____
_____
_____
_____
_____
_____
_____
_____
_____
_____
_____
_____
_____
_____
_____
_____
_____
_____
_____
_____
_____
_____
_____
_____
_____

Love was always so complex.
It knew how to make me happy
but also knew how to break my heart.
It held me yet it broke me.
That was because the love I knew
Didn't come near to His true love.
When my heart met His,
I understood that my life had yet begun.

Date: _____

Reflections: _____
_____
_____
_____
_____
_____
_____
_____
_____
_____
_____
_____
_____
_____
_____
_____
_____
_____
_____
_____
_____
_____
_____
_____
_____
_____
_____
_____
_____
_____
_____

The world tries to tell us
that beauty is only outward.
That the only way to be seen or heard
is by fitting into their "normal."
But who told them the
standard of beauty?
Because our Father made us
unique in beauty,
our shades, our sizes, our hearts
is what makes us so
fearfully and wonderfully made.

Date: _____

Reflections: _____

_____
_____
_____
_____
_____
_____
_____
_____
_____
_____
_____
_____
_____
_____
_____
_____
_____
_____
_____
_____
_____
_____
_____
_____
_____
_____
_____
_____

I once believed my happiness was enough.
That all I needed was experiences
to attain "my happy."
Oh but little did I know that when
I encountered His joy,
His everlasting joy,
how my heart will attain a forever satisfaction.
Oh, how my heart rejoices,
for "my happy" never attained a joy like this.

Date: _____

Reflections: _____

I couldn't see – my eyes veiled
but in my darkness,
I saw His Light
I saw a glimpse of what could be
this Light sat with me
It didn't speak, it didn't move
little did I know what it held.
Love…peace…joy
My life changed
and now I write and say to you
There is hope in His
Love…peace…and joy.

Date: _____

Reflections: _____

I spoke to Him in anger.
I thought a good God wouldn't
want to cause me pain.
I sat there alone
with no idea what to do next.
I cried and mourned about what life
had taken from me.
And all I could ask is "why me?"
But now I see that He emptied me
so He can fill me.
I saw pain, He saw restoration.
I lost myself and yet I found Him.

Date: _____

Reflections: _____

_____
_____
_____
_____
_____
_____
_____
_____
_____
_____
_____
_____
_____
_____
_____
_____
_____
_____
_____
_____
_____
_____
_____
_____
_____
_____
_____
_____
_____

My heart unraveled.
My eyes can see.
His Words gave me comfort.
His Joy gave me peace.
His Love paved a way.
His Presence gave me rest.
Now I walk
to help others see,
how my God can
also set you free.

Date: _____

Reflections: _____
_____
_____
_____
_____
_____
_____
_____
_____
_____
_____
_____
_____
_____
_____
_____
_____
_____
_____
_____
_____
_____
_____
_____
_____
_____
_____
_____
_____
_____
_____
_____
_____
_____
_____

A pure soul
bombarded by societal norms
embitters our hearts
forces us to fit the mold.
We yearn for hope
we yearn for peace
we cry out for love
Where do we go from here?
Look above, look within
our Maker is near.
Oh what beauty awaits for those
who declare Jesus is King.

Date: _____

Reflections: _____
_____
_____
_____
_____
_____
_____
_____
_____
_____
_____
_____
_____
_____
_____
_____
_____
_____
_____
_____
_____
_____
_____
_____
_____
_____
_____
_____
_____

Your eyes tell a story
Your silence speaks.
It's hard to believe
when life has been unfair
that faith as small as a mustard seed
is all that you need
to move those mountains from here to there.

Date: _____

Reflections: _____

_____
_____
_____
_____
_____
_____
_____
_____
_____
_____
_____
_____
_____
_____
_____
_____
_____
_____
_____
_____
_____
_____
_____
_____
_____
_____
_____
_____
_____

My burden is heavy I say
Your burden is light You say.
My soul is weary I say
You'll give me rest you say.
So I go to You and say
teach me Your ways
to be gentle and lowly in heart.

My ways are too heavy,
my thoughts too condemning,
my mind longs for rest.
Oh thank you my God
For this burden I carry
it is now yours for the keeping.

Date: _____

Reflections: _____
_____
_____
_____
_____
_____
_____
_____
_____
_____
_____
_____
_____
_____
_____
_____
_____
_____
_____
_____
_____
_____
_____
_____
_____
_____
_____
_____
_____
_____
_____

I saw Him from afar,
didn't care to seek Him
I didn't seem to care.
My heart was my compass
my thoughts were my god.
But life forced me to see,
His thoughts are higher than my thoughts
His ways are higher than my ways.
How can I withstand? How can I escape?
Life led me to You
and so now, here is where I stay.

Date: _____

Reflections: _____
_____
_____
_____
_____
_____
_____
_____
_____
_____
_____
_____
_____
_____
_____
_____
_____
_____
_____
_____
_____
_____
_____
_____
_____
_____
_____
_____
_____

The pain that you carry
is hurting your mental,
it's hurting your physical.
You speak in a rage,
you hide from your wounds
you want an escape.
I'm here to remind you
what freedom it brings,
when the pain that you carry
has no longer a say.

Date: _____

Reflections: _____
_____
_____
_____
_____
_____
_____
_____
_____
_____
_____
_____
_____
_____
_____
_____
_____
_____
_____
_____
_____
_____
_____
_____
_____
_____
_____
_____
_____
_____
_____

Face your storms.
don't let it consume.
Because our God made a promise,
that His everlasting Love
will always uphold.

Date: _____

Reflections: _____
_____
_____
_____
_____
_____
_____
_____
_____
_____
_____
_____
_____
_____
_____
_____
_____
_____
_____
_____
_____
_____
_____
_____
_____
_____
_____
_____
_____
_____

Lonely yet not alone.
Sad yet at peace.
Angry but not embittered.
Discouraged but not defeated.
Oh what a feeling it is,
to dwell in the shelter
and rest in the shadow
of the Most High.

Date: _____

Reflections: _____
_____
_____
_____
_____
_____
_____
_____
_____
_____
_____
_____
_____
_____
_____
_____
_____
_____
_____
_____
_____
_____
_____
_____
_____
_____
_____
_____
_____
_____

My identity was stolen.
My passion in question.
My purpose forgotten.
But God…
My identity recovered.
My passion ignited.
My purpose reminded.

Date: _____

Reflections: _____
_____
_____
_____
_____
_____
_____
_____
_____
_____
_____
_____
_____
_____
_____
_____
_____
_____
_____
_____
_____
_____
_____
_____
_____
_____
_____
_____
_____
_____
_____
_____
_____

The glory was too much to grasp.
A glory that only He can withstand.
I couldn't carry people's burdens,
I couldn't carry their mistakes.
I couldn't even dare,
to stand up in their place.
Only He can collect the glory
that was hidden in my hands.

Date: _____

Reflections: _____
_____
_____
_____
_____
_____
_____
_____
_____
_____
_____
_____
_____
_____
_____
_____
_____
_____
_____
_____
_____
_____
_____
_____
_____
_____
_____
_____
_____
_____
_____
_____

His safe house
here is where I run to.
When life comes to question
if my direction is true
I run to His safe house and say,
my God always comes through.

Date: _____

Reflections: _____
_____
_____
_____
_____
_____
_____
_____
_____
_____
_____
_____
_____
_____
_____
_____
_____
_____
_____
_____
_____
_____
_____
_____
_____
_____
_____
_____
_____
_____

I once believed
my words were irrelevant.
My kind gestures a waste.
Until I met a young fellow who said,
you lighted a path
that helped me to see,
I once lived in darkness
but now I can see
that the One that you worship
was the answer for me.

Date: _____

Reflections: _____
_____
_____
_____
_____
_____
_____
_____
_____
_____
_____
_____
_____
_____
_____
_____
_____
_____
_____
_____
_____
_____
_____
_____
_____
_____
_____
_____
_____
_____
_____
_____

His never-ending grace,
no one can measure.
His never-ending love,
no one can give.
His never-ending peace,
no one can provide.
How I hope that all may see
that what they are in search of
are in the Hands of our Lord Jesus Christ.

Date: _____

Reflections: _____
_____
_____
_____
_____
_____
_____
_____
_____
_____
_____
_____
_____
_____
_____
_____
_____
_____
_____
_____
_____
_____
_____
_____
_____
_____
_____
_____
_____
_____
_____
_____

How can you serve a God
that you cannot see?
How can you set your hope
on what you cannot touch?
But how can I not?
My life is a testimony.
My renewing mind is a witness.
My breath is a reminder.
My faith is my sustenance.
And yet you ask how can I believe?

Date: _____

Reflections: _____
_____
_____
_____
_____
_____
_____
_____
_____
_____
_____
_____
_____
_____
_____
_____
_____
_____
_____
_____
_____
_____
_____
_____
_____
_____
_____
_____
_____
_____

He thought of me before conception,
He formed me in my mother's womb.
He made me in His image,
He called me by my name.
He purposed me for His Glory,
so I can then proclaim,
that He is my sustainer,
my Lord and my salvation.

Date: _____

Reflections: _____
_____
_____
_____
_____
_____
_____
_____
_____
_____
_____
_____
_____
_____
_____
_____
_____
_____
_____
_____
_____
_____
_____
_____
_____
_____
_____
_____
_____
_____
_____

The fruit of the poisonous tree,
was the path I once walked on.
Anger, resentment, and bitterness
were the lens of my discernment.
The sneaky lies of the serpent
I believed to be my guide,
"Surely you will not die."
But every bite I ate,
the more I grew to hate,
the person who was becoming.
Until the person who was becoming
encountered the One True King.

Date: _____

Reflections: _____

Before the formation of creation,
Wasn't it He?
He who said "Let there be…"
The sun, moon, and the stars
the heavens, the earth and everything in between.
So why the worry and concern?
Because He who dresses the lilies
delights in the clothing of your soul.

Date: _____

Reflections: _____

_____
_____
_____
_____
_____
_____
_____
_____
_____
_____
_____
_____
_____
_____
_____
_____
_____
_____
_____
_____
_____
_____
_____
_____
_____
_____
_____

When you were in bondage,
you cried out for My saving,
so I sent you a Savior.
While you wandered in the desert,
My provision came from the heavens.
Endurance was what I was teaching,
faith was what I was building,
to lead you to the land of plenty.
Stay the course,
for what you're awaiting
is what awaits.

Date: _____

Reflections: _____

_____
_____
_____
_____
_____
_____
_____
_____
_____
_____
_____
_____
_____
_____
_____
_____
_____
_____
_____
_____
_____
_____
_____
_____
_____
_____
_____
_____

An illusion of control
is what creates the chaos in your soul.
Your mind says "I want."
Your heart says "I need."
He says "let go,"
for the certainty solely lies in the
House of the Great I Am.

Date: _____

Reflections: _____

_____
_____
_____
_____
_____
_____
_____
_____
_____
_____
_____
_____
_____
_____
_____
_____
_____
_____
_____
_____
_____
_____
_____
_____
_____
_____
_____
_____
_____
_____

Made in His image,
You were created to be.
Carefully handcrafted by the Maker's Hands.
Nothing was out of place,
no mistakes were made.
He created you with a purpose,
while promising to never leave.
Oh that you may never forget,
that you were created to never be separated
from the Love that He is in His Son demonstrated.

Date: _____

Reflections: _____
_____
_____
_____
_____
_____
_____
_____
_____
_____
_____
_____
_____
_____
_____
_____
_____
_____
_____
_____
_____
_____
_____
_____
_____
_____
_____
_____
_____
_____

I had a vision,
Of a person who was praying.
The prayer shook my heart,
a feeling…
A feeling that I have yet to find words to describe.
My skin began to radiate
A shine that no light can create.
My heart began to see
that my God was creating a new life within.

Date: _____

Reflections: _____

Don't give up.
When life tells you
your efforts are in vain,
that you deserve
all your pain.
God promises
that He will sustain,
again and again,
He will remain.

Date: _____

Reflections: _____

_____
_____
_____
_____
_____
_____
_____
_____
_____
_____
_____
_____
_____
_____
_____
_____
_____
_____
_____
_____
_____
_____
_____
_____
_____
_____
_____

In the depth of my cry,
My God heard my cry.
He saved me.
He raised me.
He gave me new life.

Date: _____

Reflections: _____
_____
_____
_____
_____
_____
_____
_____
_____
_____
_____
_____
_____
_____
_____
_____
_____
_____
_____
_____
_____
_____
_____
_____
_____
_____
_____
_____

The Lord rescues me,
The Lord sustains me,
Though I may sink,
I still stay afloat.
Though I may fall,
I still remain tall.

Date: _____

Reflections: _____
_____
_____
_____
_____
_____
_____
_____
_____
_____
_____
_____
_____
_____
_____
_____
_____
_____
_____
_____
_____
_____
_____
_____
_____
_____
_____
_____
_____
_____
_____

Behind my façade,
He sees the splendor of my soul,
He sees the beauty of it all.
He loves me with my flaws and all.

Date: _____

Reflections: _____
_____
_____
_____
_____
_____
_____
_____
_____
_____
_____
_____
_____
_____
_____
_____
_____
_____
_____
_____
_____
_____
_____
_____
_____
_____
_____
_____
_____

Our days are a shadow,
a life but a mist.
Live for today,
love for today,
take care of today.
For today is His gift.

Date: _____

Reflections: _____
_____
_____
_____
_____
_____
_____
_____
_____
_____
_____
_____
_____
_____
_____
_____
_____
_____
_____
_____
_____
_____
_____
_____
_____
_____
_____
_____
_____
_____

When it feels that the weight of my struggle,
is what's weighing me down
where does my strength come from?
I look up to the mountains,
my strength is nowhere there.
My strength comes from its Maker.
The Maker of the mountains,
the heavens,
and the earth.

Date: _____

Reflections: _____

_____
_____
_____
_____
_____
_____
_____
_____
_____
_____
_____
_____
_____
_____
_____
_____
_____
_____
_____
_____
_____
_____
_____
_____
_____
_____
_____
_____
_____
_____

*"God is within her, she will not fall;
God will help her at break of day."
Psalm 46:5*

*"Wake up, sleeper,
rise from the dead,
and Christ will shine on you."
Ephesians 5:14*

My eyes have seen,
my heart has felt
the weight of this world.
I too know,
what it's like
to be hurled
by the currents,
to be tossed and turned
by the seas.
Take heart!
He has it all figured out!
Your eyes haven't seen,
your ears haven't heard,
your mind can't conceive,
the things God has prepared
for those who love Him still.

Date: _____

Reflections: _____
_____
_____
_____
_____
_____
_____
_____
_____
_____
_____
_____
_____
_____
_____
_____
_____
_____
_____
_____
_____
_____
_____
_____
_____
_____
_____
_____
_____
_____

My heart is breaking
my tears are what feeds
the hollow of my soul.
Oh how I may find relief
in Your console!
My God, My Lord,
Your Word is the glory of it all!
You comfort my heart, you watch over my soul.
My heart is all yours Lord,
Give me rest for my soul.

Date: _____

Reflections: _____

_____
_____
_____
_____
_____
_____
_____
_____
_____
_____
_____
_____
_____
_____
_____
_____
_____
_____
_____
_____
_____
_____
_____
_____
_____
_____
_____

Distressed,
And in my sigh,
He made me a promise to abide always by my side.

Date: _____

Reflections: _____
_____
_____
_____
_____
_____
_____
_____
_____
_____
_____
_____
_____
_____
_____
_____
_____
_____
_____
_____
_____
_____
_____
_____
_____
_____
_____
_____
_____

Only for a season,
hang on for this reason…
Trouble may come
but do not despair,
Rejoice!
The sun is arising,
joy is on the horizon
your blessing is near.

Date: _____

Reflections: _____

In stillness, He is very near.
What may look like His absence,
it's Him in His doing.
Oh how wonderful it is to envelope
ourselves in stillness.
To bask in God's doing while we rest in faith.
May the God of the heavens and the earth
cover you while you lie in waiting
for His love to forever embrace you.

Date: _____

Reflections: _____

In the stillness of the silence,
I heard my name.
Was it He?
The He who died for me?
He found beauty in my name,
although I found only shame.
The goodness of His grace
the mercy of His love,
was the embrace
that enlightened my ways.

Date: _____

Reflections: _____

_____
_____
_____
_____
_____
_____
_____
_____
_____
_____
_____
_____
_____
_____
_____
_____
_____
_____
_____
_____
_____
_____
_____
_____
_____
_____
_____
_____
_____

In my hopelessness, He gave me hope.

Date: _____

Reflections: _____
_____
_____
_____
_____
_____
_____
_____
_____
_____
_____
_____
_____
_____
_____
_____
_____
_____
_____
_____
_____
_____
_____
_____
_____
_____
_____
_____
_____

When life overwhelmed me,
He was there.
When I saw no hope,
He was there.
When I had no will to fight,
He was there.
And just when I thought there was nothing left
I took ahold of His garment,
power came out of Him.
It was like a new breath…
like nothing I ever experienced.
This is what it is, to feel reborn.

Date: _____

Reflections: _____
_____
_____
_____
_____
_____
_____
_____
_____
_____
_____
_____
_____
_____
_____
_____
_____
_____
_____
_____
_____
_____
_____
_____
_____
_____
_____
_____
_____
_____

My prayers were wordless groans,
my lips too broken to speak.
Little did I know,
that my wordless groans
were the permission for Him to speak.

Date: _____

Reflections: _____
_____
_____
_____
_____
_____
_____
_____
_____
_____
_____
_____
_____
_____
_____
_____
_____
_____
_____
_____
_____
_____
_____
_____
_____
_____
_____

There was beauty in the pain,
a comfort in my cry.
I didn't understand,
I couldn't see why.
It was all for my good
and now I see why.

Date: _____

Reflections: _____
_____
_____
_____
_____
_____
_____
_____
_____
_____
_____
_____
_____
_____
_____
_____
_____
_____
_____
_____
_____
_____
_____
_____
_____
_____
_____
_____
_____
_____

He sought me
when I wasn't seeking.
He embraced me
when I wasn't feeling.
He whispered
when I wasn't hearing.
My rejection was His pursuit.
Until my life became His fruit.

Date: _____

Reflections: _____

_____
_____
_____
_____
_____
_____
_____
_____
_____
_____
_____
_____
_____
_____
_____
_____
_____
_____
_____
_____
_____
_____
_____
_____
_____

Thank you my God,
for what you have done.
You gave me new life,
You gave me a new hope.
Oh how I rejoice,
for Your love is what carries me through and through.

Date: _____

Reflections: _____
_____
_____
_____
_____
_____
_____
_____
_____
_____
_____
_____
_____
_____
_____
_____
_____
_____
_____
_____
_____
_____
_____
_____
_____
_____
_____
_____
_____
_____

The marching made no sense to me,
my enemy seemed so much bigger than me.
My silence confounded me,
yet His Word is what guided me.
"Go" is what He said to me.
But my fear took ahold of me,
"Let go of me!"
And the walls came down right in front of me.

Date: _____

Reflections: _____
_____
_____
_____
_____
_____
_____
_____
_____
_____
_____
_____
_____
_____
_____
_____
_____
_____
_____
_____
_____
_____
_____
_____
_____
_____
_____
_____
_____
_____

My anxious thoughts led me to question
His intention,
But never was He put off by my questions.
He openly received my uncertainty,
and answered me certainly,
don't worry about anything;
yet pray about everything.

Date: _____

Reflections: _____
_____
_____
_____
_____
_____
_____
_____
_____
_____
_____
_____
_____
_____
_____
_____
_____
_____
_____
_____
_____
_____
_____
_____
_____
_____
_____
_____
_____
_____
_____

Where do I go from here?
Stirred by my question,
welcomed by my fear,
He parted the seas,
He put me at ease.

Date: _____

Reflections: _____
_____
_____
_____
_____
_____
_____
_____
_____
_____
_____
_____
_____
_____
_____
_____
_____
_____
_____
_____
_____
_____
_____
_____
_____
_____
_____
_____
_____

In His Shadow is where I lay.
When the world seems chaotic
and satan's words are hypnotic,
I lay in His Shadow,
for in His Shadow is where I know,
that I can dwell in the safety
of the shelter of the Most High.

Date: _____

Reflections: _____
_____
_____
_____
_____
_____
_____
_____
_____
_____
_____
_____
_____
_____
_____
_____
_____
_____
_____
_____
_____
_____
_____
_____
_____
_____
_____
_____
_____

You woke me out my slumber,
you woke me out my sleep.
You told me there was life,
a new life awaiting.
So I took your invitation
and made the declaration,
that you are my Lord,
my God and my salvation.

Date: _____

Reflections: _____

_____
_____
_____
_____
_____
_____
_____
_____
_____
_____
_____
_____
_____
_____
_____
_____
_____
_____
_____
_____
_____
_____
_____
_____
_____
_____
_____
_____
_____
_____

Rejoice!
He who clothed you with salvation!
Rejoice!
He who covered you with the robe of righteousness!
Rejoice!
For your soul rejoices in the Lord.

Date: _____

Reflections: _____

_____
_____
_____
_____
_____
_____
_____
_____
_____
_____
_____
_____
_____
_____
_____
_____
_____
_____
_____
_____
_____
_____
_____
_____
_____
_____
_____
_____

He is faithful to forgive,
though your sins want you to believe,
"You are not good enough,
you will never be."
The lies that it feeds
are so easy to believe,
but God says
your sins are covered,
The Word has you hovered.
The Word became flesh,
so that you can confess
and freely profess
"There is now no condemnation
for those who are in Jesus Christ."

Date: _____

Reflections: _____
_____
_____
_____
_____
_____
_____
_____
_____
_____
_____
_____
_____
_____
_____
_____
_____
_____
_____
_____
_____
_____
_____
_____
_____
_____
_____
_____
_____
_____

A woman after God's own heart,
is what I'll be.
Shaped by His character,
is what He'll decree.
I'll set my heart out to Him,
I'll trust in His ways
all of my days.
For a woman after God's own heart
is what I'll set my heart to be.

Date: _____

Reflections: _____
_____
_____
_____
_____
_____
_____
_____
_____
_____
_____
_____
_____
_____
_____
_____
_____
_____
_____
_____
_____
_____
_____
_____
_____
_____
_____
_____

He set my foot on a rock,
and gave me a firm place to stand.
He gave me His commands
and took ahold of my hands,
"I will go with you,
I promise to never leave you,
do not be afraid
or dismayed,
for I am your God
and I will forever be with you."

Date: _____

Reflections: _____

_____
_____
_____
_____
_____
_____
_____
_____
_____
_____
_____
_____
_____
_____
_____
_____
_____
_____
_____
_____
_____
_____
_____
_____
_____
_____
_____

The growth that partakes in our soul
is what we should give Him full control,
for our hearts knows not where to go.
He builds us,
He grows us,
He guides us,
He sustains us,
He rewards us.
So while our hearts may deceive us,
let it be Him who reprieves us.

Date: _____

Reflections: _____

Be patient.
Be strong.
Do not be disheartened,
do not let your hearts be hardened.
For God's promises
are faithful and true,
for He promises to carry you through.

Date: _____

Reflections: _____

Don't be deceived,
by what you superficially see.
Titles, wealth, and power
hold temporal successes
with many distresses.
Nevertheless, may you be impressed
by His faithfulness,
His sovereignty
and power.
For His Words are unchanging and forever lasting.

Date: _____

Reflections: _____
_____
_____
_____
_____
_____
_____
_____
_____
_____
_____
_____
_____
_____
_____
_____
_____
_____
_____
_____
_____
_____
_____
_____
_____
_____
_____

He came into this world
so you can get to see,
the love that He held
since before they ate of that tree.
He carried your shame,
He held out His hands
He became the sin
that was His demand.
For judgement needed his say,
it cried out for justice,
but it would never be sustained
by the efforts of those who remained.
So He sent His Son to take up
for those He ordained,
to be the sons and the daughters
to live a life unrestrained.

Date: _____

Reflections: _____
_____
_____
_____
_____
_____
_____
_____
_____
_____
_____
_____
_____
_____
_____
_____
_____
_____
_____
_____
_____
_____
_____
_____
_____
_____
_____
_____
_____

It felt weak and foolish
to humble myself to selfless service.
But when I looked to the cross,
to the One who left the riches of heaven
to pay the ransom for many.
Now I consider it plenty
the reward that it gives
to walk in the service of many.

Date: _____

Reflections: _____

He set a path before me.
He asked me which do you choose?
There are two paths to walk on,
so pay attention carefully.
One leads to death
and the other leads to life.
While it may seem like a given,
the path of the dead
seemed so elaborate and luxurious
and the path to life
seemed so narrow and mysterious.
However, I set my eyes before Him
and said where you go I will go,
for your path is The Way I choose.

Date: _____

Reflections: _____

_____
_____
_____
_____
_____
_____
_____
_____
_____
_____
_____
_____
_____
_____
_____
_____
_____
_____
_____
_____
_____
_____
_____
_____
_____
_____
_____
_____
_____

While you pushed through
your cry and your struggle,
you were led to believe
you were destined for many troubles.

But here's the Good News!
He came to set you free,
from the lies of the enemy's schemes.
He came to give you life
to enjoy it to the full.
Come on! Grab ahold of His promises,
because they will surely keep you
and greatly bless you.

Date: _____

Reflections: _____
_____
_____
_____
_____
_____
_____
_____
_____
_____
_____
_____
_____
_____
_____
_____
_____
_____
_____
_____
_____
_____
_____
_____
_____
_____
_____
_____
_____
_____

He set your heart for a purpose.
He set your mind to understand.
He set a path for you to walk on.
His Word remains your guarantee,
to worry not,
for your destiny is His decree.

Date: _____

Reflections: _____

_____
_____
_____
_____
_____
_____
_____
_____
_____
_____
_____
_____
_____
_____
_____
_____
_____
_____
_____
_____
_____
_____
_____
_____
_____

You are the work of His Hands,
the beauty of His image.
You were made to love Him,
you were made from His love.
Let your hearts rejoice,
let your hearts not be troubled.
For His unfailing love surrounds us
and forevermore we shall confide in His love.

Date: _____

Reflections: _____
_____
_____
_____
_____
_____
_____
_____
_____
_____
_____
_____
_____
_____
_____
_____
_____
_____
_____
_____
_____
_____
_____
_____
_____
_____
_____
_____
_____

My soul cried out for mercy,
my actions were too unworthy.
My mind called out my sins,
my heart felt all of life's worries.

My child, oh child, God said
your sins are forgiven,
your soul has been cleansed,
you are no longer condemned.

So rest up my child,
that the work of the cross
has freed you instead.

Date: _____

Reflections: _____
_____
_____
_____
_____
_____
_____
_____
_____
_____
_____
_____
_____
_____
_____
_____
_____
_____
_____
_____
_____
_____
_____
_____
_____
_____
_____
_____
_____
_____

As I lay my eyes to sleep,
I can't help but to think,
of His goodness and how it saved me.
His mercy has been unchanging,
His grace is forever unending.
So as I lay my eyes to sleep,
I can't help but to see
how He has always remained alongside of me.

Date: _____

Reflections: _____
_____
_____
_____
_____
_____
_____
_____
_____
_____
_____
_____
_____
_____
_____
_____
_____
_____
_____
_____
_____
_____
_____
_____
_____
_____
_____
_____
_____
_____

At my lowest
I saw nothing but my pain,
life seem to look at me with disdain.
I felt no glory in His name,
I prayed and prayed
until no words remained.
"Where are you?" I claimed.
Can't you hear my claims?
I felt so detained,
Your Word said you can break these chains,
will You please deliver me from these pains?

My daughter, my child,
I sat beside you in your pain,
I heard all your cries.
I was building your heart to walk on
a path to where others will see you rise.
So in exchange for all your chains,
receive My peace, My joy, My never ending love
for these will always remain.

Date: _____

Reflections: _____

_____
_____
_____
_____
_____
_____
_____
_____
_____
_____
_____
_____
_____
_____
_____
_____
_____
_____
_____
_____
_____
_____
_____
_____
_____
_____
_____
_____

God that you may continue to speak
to all those who seek.
That You will continue to strengthen
to all those who may question
their purpose or Your intentions.
May You continue to show them Your Ways
May they see Your Love and Your Grace.
For Your love extends
as far as the east is from the west.
Thank you Lord Jesus,
because you have given them life,
life to the full.

Amen.

Date: _____

Reflections: _____
_____
_____
_____
_____
_____
_____
_____
_____
_____
_____
_____
_____
_____
_____
_____
_____
_____
_____
_____
_____
_____
_____
_____
_____
_____
_____
_____
_____

"For I am convinced that neither death nor life, neither angels nor demons, neither the present nor the future, nor any powers, neither height nor depth, nor anything else in all creation, will be able to separate us from the love of God that is in Christ Jesus our Lord."
Romans 8:38-39

*"The Lord bless you and keep you;
The Lord make His face shine upon you,
And be gracious to you;
The Lord lift up His countenance upon you,
And give you peace."
Numbers 6:24-26*

Made in United States
Orlando, FL
08 December 2022